THE MUSIC OF GRAMMAR

Grammar in Verses

Pooja Mandla

BookLeaf
Publishing

India | USA | UK

Made with ❤ on the BookLeaf Publishing Platform
www.bookleafpub.in
www.bookleafpub.com

Dedication

To my **family**, my strength and light,
Whose love has led me through each night.
Your faith and warmth, so calm, so deep,
Have sown the dreams I wished to keep.

To my **students**, with hearts so bright,
You turned my lessons into light.
Your laughter, questions, and eager eyes,
Made grammar's rules a sweet surprise.

May these verses gently show,
That even rules can bloom and glow.
For when grammar and poetry blend,
Learning becomes a lifelong friend.

Preface

Words can dance, and sentences can sing,
Grammar has rhythm in everything.
From nouns that stand to verbs that fly,
Figures of speech can reach the sky.

Language is more than a tool for communication; it is the music of thought, the rhythm of expression, and the soul of imagination. Over the years of teaching and learning English, I often felt that grammar, though essential, is perceived as something mechanical and lifeless. The idea of this book was born from the desire to change that belief to make grammar sing, smile, and stay.

"Grammar in Verse" brings together the rules of language and the beauty of poetry. Each poem in this book explains a concept from the Parts of Speech to the Figures of Speech in a way that's simple, rhythmic, and memorable. The first stanza defines the idea, while the second illustrates it with examples, turning each lesson into a lyrical experience.

This book is designed to accompany learners through their entire school journey from Grade 1 to Grade 12. It grows with the reader, becoming a lifelong companion that transforms grammar from a subject to a source of joy. Teachers can use it to bring creativity into the classroom, while students can explore the wonder of words beyond rules and rote learning.

May these verses help every learner discover that grammar, when blended with poetry, is not just about correctness; it's about connection, creativity, and the art of expression.

Pooja Mandla

Acknowledgements

To my family,

for being my constant source of strength and love- your patience, faith, and quiet encouragement have been the wind beneath my words. Every rhyme I wrote carries a touch of your support and warmth.

To my students,

who inspired every page of this book —
your questions, curiosity, and enthusiasm gave life to grammar and rhythm to poetry. You are the reason this dream found its form.

And to my readers,

thank you for opening these pages with an open heart.
May each verse in this book make you feel the joy of learning,
the beauty of language,
and the magic that happens when grammar begins to sing.

1. THE MUSIC OF GRAMMAR

Section I: Grammar in Poetry

The Music of Grammar

Grammar's a heartbeat, steady and kind,
It carries the symphony that lies in the mind.
It hums in our whispers, it soars in our cries,
It dances in laughter, it softens goodbyes.

Not chains to confine us, but wings to soar,
It opens up worlds, both near and more.
It shapes every voice, both gentle and true,
The beauty of grammar is the music of you.

2. Section II: The Parts of Speech

The Melody of Noun

Transition to Noun

Before we can sing or whisper or call,
We need the names that hold it all.
Let us begin with the noun, so true,
The world is alive because it names you.
A **noun is a name**, the start of all sound,
It tells what's above and what's around.
It names each joy, each tear, each place,
It gives the world its form and face.
Proper Nouns stand proud and tall,
Like *India, Lucy, London Hall.*
Common Nouns we see each day
A bird, a child, the sunbeam's ray.
Collective Nouns bring groups in sight
A bunch of stars, a troop of light.
Abstract Nouns are soft as air
Dreams, hope, love that's always there.

Material Nouns build all we see

Gold, wood, silver, sea.

So sing, dear noun, your naming tune

You give the world its voice and bloom!

3. The Magic of Pronoun

Transition to Pronoun

Nouns give a name to all we see,
People, places, things, and thee.
When names repeat too much in line,
Pronouns step in to shine and rhyme!

A **Pronoun** stands where a noun has been,
It keeps our speech smooth and clean.
It shows who, what, or whose it may be,
And makes our words flow naturally.
Personal Pronouns - *I, you, he, she, we, they,*
Possessive Pronouns - *mine, yours, ours ,hooray!*
Demonstrative Pronouns -*this, that, these, those,*
Reflexive Pronouns -*myself, yourself; it shows.*
Interrogative Pronouns- *who, what, which we ask,*
Relative Pronouns- *who, whose, that* complete the task.
So pronouns dance, both near and far,
With nouns they sparkle, like stars that are!

4. The Dance Verb and Adverbs

Transition to Verb and Adverb

Nouns and pronouns give names that stay,
They show us who or what in play.
*But **actions** need **verbs** to leap and move,*
*And **adverbs** add style, their rhythm and groove!*
A **verb** shows action, what we do,
It runs, it jumps, it laughs, it flew.
It tells us what happens, big or small,
It's the heartbeat of words, the life of all.
Action Verbs- run, write, sing, play,
Linking Verbs- is, am, are, they say.
Helping Verbs-has, do, will, can,
They join the action, a verb's best plan.
An adverb tells us how, when, or where,
It adds to verbs with style and flair.
Quickly, softly, yesterday, near,
They color the action, make meaning clear.
Together they dance, verb and adverb bright,
Bringing our sentences rhythm and light. ☼

5. The Magic of Adjectives

Transition to Adjectives
Verbs show the action, adverbs show how,
They make our sentences dance and wow.
But nouns need colors, details to prize,
So adjectives step in to beautify the skies!

An **adjective** adds color and light,
It paints the noun and makes words bright.
It tells what kind, how many, or which,
Turning plain speech into a poetic pitch.
Descriptive- *beautiful, tall, bright, or small,*
Quantitative - *some, few, many, all.*
Demonstrative -*this, that, these, those,*
Possessive -*my, your, our, it shows.*
Interrogative -*which, what, whose we ask,*
Giving the nouns their shining mask.
Adjectives dance, a colorful spree,
They make every sentence a sight to see! ☼

6. The Binding Conjunction

Transition to Conjunction
But words alone may drift apart,
We need a bridge to join each heart.
Conjunctions arrive with hands that bind,
Uniting thoughts, both yours and mine.

A **conjunction** is friendship, it ties word to word,
It gathers the voices so all can be heard.
It balances choices, it offers a way,
It links night to morning, and work to the play.

It holds things together, both little and vast,
It stitches the future, it mends up the past.
Without its embrace, speech falls into two,
Conjunctions remind us: "I join, I renew."

7. The Guiding Preposition

Transition to Preposition

Still, we need guides to show us where,
A map through space, through time, through air.
Prepositions step in with a gentle hand,
They place every word where it ought to stand.

A **preposition** is compass, pointing the way,
It tells us of "*under,*" "*beyond,*" or "*away.*"
It shows how the pieces of meaning align,
It charts out the course in a steady design.

It walks with precision, it steadies the ground,
It whispers directions where order is found.
It places our language in balance and song,
Prepositions guide us, they carry us strong.

8. The Sudden Interjection

Transition to Interjection

Sometimes words burst out like flame,
Unplanned, unpolished, yet never the same.
Interjections arrive with laughter or cries,
The sudden emotions no tongue can disguise.

An **interjection** is lightning, it strikes with surprise,
It shouts in our joy, or it weeps in our sighs.
It leaps from the heart, both tender and wild,
The voice of the moment, unguarded, unstyled.

It startles the silence, it quickens the air,
It's honest and human, beyond all compare.
Though small in its form, it's mighty and true,
The interjection speaks what words cannot do.

9. The Articles Touch

Transition to Article

Now last we meet the quiet guide,
So small in size, yet dignified.
The article comes with a subtle role,
To shape the meaning and make it whole.

An **Article** whispers of "**a,**" "**an,**" or "**the,**"
It frames every noun with quiet decree.
It signals the certain, the known, the near,
Or opens the path when many appear.

It sharpens the focus, it narrows the light,
It softens the edges, it sets things right.
Though tiny in presence, it carries much weight,
The article steadies what nouns create.

10. Section III: The Literary Devices
Simile- A Bridge of "Like" and "As"

Section III: The Literary Devices
Transition to Simile

To compare is a poet's delight,
It bridges two worlds with gentle light.
Let us begin with the simile's song,
Where likeness makes language forever strong.
A **Simile** compares **two unlike things** with ease,
Using like or as to charm and please.
It says as brave as a lion's roar,
Or soft like waves on a silver shore.
It paints with words, both near and far,
Her eyes shine bright like the evening star.
It helps us see through poet's eyes,
How language blooms, how beauty lies.

11. Metaphor- The Mirror of Meaning

Transition to Metaphor

But sometimes words go deeper still,
They change the world by force of will.
A metaphor steps in, bold and strong,
Turning plain speech into golden song.

A **Metaphor** speaks without like or as,
It doesn't compare; it simply becomes what it has.
It joins two worlds, both near and far,
And shows what things truly are.
It says life is a journey, we walk each mile,
It says hope is a candle that burns with a smile.
It makes our thoughts both deep and wide,
Where truth and feeling gently collide.
It gives new wings to the words we store,
It turns plain speech to something more.
A metaphor shines through joy and strife-
It is the soul and song of life.

12. The Spirit of Personification

Transition to Personification

But sometimes the lifeless may rise and sing,
The world takes on voices, the night wears a ring.
Personification whispers its part,
Breathing in life, giving soul to the heart.

Personification gives **life** to the **still**,
It lends heart to the stone, and voice to the hill.
It means when we say the wind softly sighs,
Or the angry storm shouts across the skies.

The river remembers, the mountains can dream,
The lamp grows weary, the stars softly gleam.
It fills the world with human grace-
Where even silence finds a face.

13. The Power of Alliteration

Transition to Alliteration

When sounds repeat like footsteps near,
A rhythm is born for the heart to hear.
Alliteration dances with echo and chime,
A melody woven in language and rhyme.

The sound starts softly, it circles, it sings,
It beats in the words like the flutter of wings.
It gathers the letters, repeating their song,
It makes simple phrases grow steady and strong.

It tickles the tongue, it quickens the pace,
It shines in the verse with a playful grace.
Alliteration whispers, it sharpens the ear,
It makes every sentence more vibrant, more clear.

14. The Strength of Repetition

Transition to Repetition

But sometimes a word must echo again,
To deepen the meaning, to sharpen the pen.
Repetition steps in with a steady refrain,
Its echoes remind us, its voice will remain.

Repetition is when words come again,
To touch the heart, to ease the pain.
A thought repeated becomes a friend,
Its echo stays till the very end.
It reminds, it comforts, it helps us feel,
It turns simple truth into something real.

Like "Hope will rise, hope will stay," we say,
And those gentle words light up our way.
They steady our hearts, they calm the fear,
They bring distant dreams a little near.
In every refrain, there's healing and grace-
Repetition gives strength, a warm embrace.

15. Exaggeration of Hyperbole

Transition to Hyperbole
And when the truth cannot hold our delight,
We stretch it beyond the day and the night.
Hyperbole thunders with glorious might,
Exaggeration blazing, a fire so bright.

Hyperbole means saying much more than is true,
To show what we feel in a brighter hue.
A mountain of sorrow, a river of tears,
A laughter that rings through endless years.
A heart so heavy it can hardly breathe,
A joy so vast you'd never believe.

It paints our emotions in colours so wide,
It shows what we carry deep inside.
Not meant to be real, but meant to be felt,
It softens the heart where truth has dwelt.
With every wild image, it helps us see —
The beauty of feelings through hyperbole.

16. The Balance of Oxymoron

Transition to Oxymoron

At times two opposites meet in embrace,
Contradictions dance with a curious grace.
Oxymoron whispers with paradox true,
Two clashing words make meaning anew.

An **Oxymoron** joins the clash of two extremes,
It blends the opposites, or so it seems.
It lives in contrast;both dark and bright,
A pairing of words that puzzle the sight.
It shows how meanings can twist and align,
Creating a thought both sharp and divine.

Examples abound in language's art-
A bitter sweet memory, a deafening heart.
Freezing fire, living dead, silent roar,
Pretty ugly face and endless shore.
It shocks the mind, yet makes it clear,
How opposites together can both appear.

17. The Voice of Onomatopoeia

Transition to Onomatopoeia

Some words don't just tell, they echo the sound,
They mimic the noise of the world all around.
Onomatopoeia speaks bold and clear,
It lets every sound be alive to the ear.

It's crackle and whisper, it's murmur and roar,
It's bang at the window, it's knock at the door.
It's drip of the raindrop, it's buzz of the bee,
It's howl of the night wind, it's crash of the sea.

It makes every echo a word we can say,
It carries the world in a playful display.
It turns sound to language, both gentle and strong,
Onomatopoeia is music in song.

18. The Twist of Transferred Epithed

Transition to Transferred Epithet

But sometimes the feeling will softly misplace,
It shifts from the soul to an object's face.
Transferred epithet moves with a poet's art,
Giving things outside what lives in the heart.

A transferred epithet shifts the sense around,
Where feelings of humans in objects are found.
It lends our emotions to things we describe,
And paints dull phrases with life's own vibe.

A sleepless night, a joyous day,
A lazy morning, a cruel way.
A happy breeze, a lonely road,
A weary smile where sorrow showed.
It swaps our moods with what we see—
That's transferred epithet's poetry!

19. The Flow of Enjabment

Transition to Enjambment
Sometimes a thought won't end with the line,
It spills to the next, in a flow so fine.
Enjambment runs forward, refusing to stay,
It carries the reader along its way.

The line breaks too soon, yet meaning flows on,
The pause is delayed though the words are gone.
It quickens the pace, it lengthens the breath,
It chases the thought through silence and depth.

It tumbles like rivers, it rushes with streams,
It bends every sentence, it carries our dreams.
It breaks every wall where the rhythm might part,
Enjambment is freedom, a poet's bold art.

20. The Play of Pun

Transition to Pun

Sometimes words play with double disguise,
A twist in their meaning delights the eyes.
Pun is the joker, the clever one,
It tickles the tongue with laughter and fun.

It's wordplay with sparkle, it dances, it teases,
It juggles with meanings in ways that it pleases.
It sharpens the wit, it startles the ear,
It turns simple speech into laughter sincere.

It may make us groan, it may make us smile,
It carries the joke with a twist all the while.
Though playful in tone, it dazzles the mind,
The **Pun** is a treasure for poets to find.

21. The contrast of Antithesis

Transition to Antithesis

But to close, we must balance the night and the day,
The dark and the light in a single display.
Antithesis teaches in mirrored release,
Opposites standing in structured peace.

Antithesis balances ideas that oppose,
It places two thoughts where difference shows.
It sharpens the meaning through contrast clear,
And makes what we say more strong and sincere.

Speech is silver, but silence is gold,
To err is human, to forgive is bold.
Many are called, but few are chosen,
Give every man thy ear, but voice to none.
It's thought against thought, both side by side,
Where truth and its shadow together reside.